The Edge of Wales

by

Jack Walkaholic

The Starting Post

Day One, Chepstow - Newport, January 1st 2023

The train screeched to a halt, jolting me back to the present—Chepstow. No turning back now. Ten years of rattling about in my skull, like a pebble in a tumble dryer, a faint echo amid the everyday hustle and bustle. The Wales Coast Path lay ahead, a promise of natural wonders and adventures to come. Granite cliffs towered majestically, bearing witness to the ceaseless rhythm of waves crashing against their unyielding embrace. Sea walls guarded against the relentless tides, while beaches whispered secrets of the past with every grain of sand. My boots thumped along the concrete platform, a nervous drumbeat against the quiet of the station.

My original plan was to do this when I retired. However, COVID taught me not to take things for granted, do things today as tomorrow is not guaranteed. So here I am on New Year's Day, wandering the streets of Chepstow. The goal is to walk the whole Wales Coast Path in a year; it's 870 miles long, the ups and downs are more than going up Everest 3 times. Today, I'm pushing my limits, seeing how much ground I can cover before the short winter day fades. I haven't walked in this area before and I'm more used to mountains than seafronts.

The Severn Bridge

I can navigate a mountain without too much trouble; I've climbed Snowden in a gale that could peel paint off a sheep but just going from the station to the start point was my first error of judgement. I followed the way markers and ended up going away from the start— lesson one learned. After a few extra paces, I found the start on the bank of the River Wye.

It's 9am and most of the world is asleep. The Old Chepstow Bridge is just a few metres away and marks the border with England. Chepstow Castle (well worth a visit) is just around the corner. Today is around 30 miles to walk and I need to get moving. The compulsory selfie fest at the start, followed by a meander through the back streets of Chepstow starts this walk. This isn't too bad; the weather is dry and the first few miles disappear without a hitch. In no time, I can see the Severn Bridge and it's about half an hour away. I've walked over it in the past; walking across the bridge is a different experience. Not one of the more popular walks of Wales but it should be. I walk under the A48 and the traffic thuds overhead like a herd of angry buffaloes. I find myself in a field of cows. I'm not afraid of cows.

The smell of damp earth clings to my nostrils, my legs were anchors in the thick mud, I'm helpless and motionless. A rumble of hooves grows louder, as the whole herd runs toward me. Thirty of the biggest, baddest bovines this side of the M5 charge my way. A shiver runs down my spine. Might be time to rethink

The Statue of The Lava Fisherman at
Black Rock

my stance on cows. I swear I can hear them mooing. "Lunch is served."

Thankfully, a friendly jogger with a particularly ferocious looking terrier comes to my rescue.The dog barks and snarls at the cows, who wisely decide that I'm not on the menu after all. I scramble over the gate and rejoin the path feeling like I just cheated death.

Before I know it I'm at Black Rock, this is a viewing area for both bridges, a statue of the Lava Rock Fishermen and a pretty good place to see a sunset.

Onward to the Prince of Wales Bridge, passing the Severn Tunnel Entrance. The Prince of Wales Bridge is the second longest bridge in the UK at an impressive 5,128 metres. Passing under it, again the clunk clunk of lorries and the clomp clomp of the cars sound like a rave above my head. With the traffic making their way between the two countries.

The rest of the day is a blur of wind, rain, hail and mud. The path sticks to the sea wall like a bulldog to its chew toy. Rain creates ponds in places, mud pools in others. With every footstep I take, I repeat my mantra "don't slip", as help is a long way away. The hail hits me in a sideways direction, I'm relieved when the path gives up the sea wall at Gold Cliff. It decides to take a path through a field. Well, it should be a field but it's more like a paddy field, with a squelch squelch underfoot. It didn't take long for me to turn around and decide to stick to the road. A loop around Uskmouth, passing the

The East Usk Lighthouse

East Usk Lighthouse, my first power plant and I realise the daylight has gone. The path goes back to the sea wall at this point but I'm not confident enough to go puddle plodding in the dark. I stick to the road through an industrial estate. I make sure I visit the Newport Transporter Bridge, before retracing my steps and continuing to the road bridge at Spittles Point.

Newport Transporter Bridge

Newport - Penarth, January 6th 2023

My second day on the Wales Coast Path felt like two halves of a city sandwich: Newport's rough-and-tumble filling contrasting with Cardiff's smooth, modern sheen. My patient sister dropped me off back at Newport, coffee and cake fueling my resolve to navigate the potholes and car parks of the city's industrial outskirts.

Newport, for all its unpolished charm, offered a backstreet safari. Leaping over cracks and dodging impatient drivers, I eventually escaped the city proper and reached the West Usk Lighthouse. This squat sentinel with its sister that I'd passed about 10 miles ago, marks the entrance to the River Usk, once a bustling coal export channel. Now, it stood silent witness to the tide's rhythm.

Back on the sea wall, a humble grassy mound crowned with raindrop jewels. I waddled like a tipsy hippopotamus, each step a test of the mud's hidden depths. My phone's map app claims the path travels through the water treatment plant, but the signs point through the streets of Splott. If I miss a way marker here, I won't know where to rejoin the path, the streets are like a labyrinth.

Finally, victory! I emerged unscathed at the legendary Magic Roundabout, this circus of concentric lanes and road signs stacked into geometric shapes.

11   *Cardiff Millennium Centre*

Emerging from the roundabout, I followed the sleek, sinuous canal towards Cardiff Bay. The Millennium Center, a slate clad zeppelin, dominated the scene. Marina stroll, barrage crossing – check and check.

The day's grand finale awaited, Paget Road. After walking mainly on the flat for 2 days, this is the first steep incline I've had to tackle, my legs wobble like jelly on a hotplate. A local shopper huffed ahead, a carrier bag in each hand, grunting with every step he took, he offered encouraging advice, "Almost There!" My heart thumped like a drum solo, pounding a victory march. "Yeah!" I laughed, he had no idea how far I had left to go. Up I go, with each step my boots feeling heavier, a circle of seagulls above me, like vultures waiting for me to fall but then the crest. The battle against gravity is over and my feet feel lighter than a helium balloon with a free lifetime supply of laughter for a few steps. The world unfolded before me like a sequin-studded disco ball. Penarth Pier below me, with the sea glittering like a diamond, I nearly choked on my own hyperventilation. I'd conquered this hill, it felt like the tourists below applauded and gasped. Probably mistaking me for a mountain goat sporting a particularly fetching backpack, I took a triumphant bow. The path stretched on, an endless buffet of adventure. I walked, I climbed and crushed it, but now it was time to call it a day.

13   *Penarth Pier*

About Me

It's about time I introduced myself: Hi, I'm Jack, comfortably in my fifties with the build of a bear—yes, I'm carrying a little extra weight but I wear it well. My work keeps me on my feet, quite literally. In my daily work routine, I walk approximately 30,000 steps, equivalent to 14 miles, on a relentless concrete floor. Alongside my colleagues, they ensure that the workday is a collaborative and lighthearted environment, striking the right balance between work and play, ensuring that I don't take anything too seriously. It's fair to say that nearly every day, I'm clocking an impressive number of miles. This isn't just about hiking; it's about proving something to myself. Can a 50-year-old man with a few extra pounds still take on a challenge like this?

I'm a keen photographer who learned the art of capturing light before the digital age. I enjoy walking up mountains to find gorgeous views and preserve them. The photos in this book aren't the usual always sunny, fluffy pictures you normally find in books. Instead, it's the reality of what I had on the day. These days the camera rarely makes an appearance: the lighter Swiss Army knife-gadgets, my phone, replaces my camera, my map, and my wallet.

This walk is crammed into weekends, holidays and any days off I can muster. Forget lounging on the couch. My adventures come with a sweat covered face, a

Treading the Boardwalks

backpack and my phone. It's my way of escaping the everyday humdrum, the dreams that tend to gather dust in the corners of our lives.

Last October, something shifted. A hint of an idea morphed into a full-blown obsession: the Wales Coast Path, 870 miles of wild beauty calling my name. It became my Everest, a challenge filling my soul with a restlessness I couldn't ignore. I was oblivious to what was going on in the world around me. On Christmas day, I was asked "Do you want any sprouts?" but my response was "Do you think Chepstow to Newport is too far for a first day?" I was too excited about my upcoming hike to care about anything else.

Admittedly, my planning wasn't exactly Napoleon-esque. My total thought was 870 miles divided by 50 weeks is a very easy 16 miles a week, I can do that! Maps, yes, I love them – I spent hours swiping around to see if the green broken line is better than the red broken line and I didn't see the solid blue line there, that's a 4 mile detour. My "master plan" involved more day dreaming and wishful thinking than logistics. The real challenge, the one that kept me up at night, was figuring out the daily dance between finish points and start points. How do you navigate this, week after week, without getting caught in a logistical tango?

I'm not interested in creating a false impression or flattering image of myself. I want to write this book with honesty and integrity, a true representation of my

Flat Holm, early morning

experience and to reflect the reality of who I am and what I have been through.

So, here I am, the dreamer, swapping work boots for walking boots, hi viz for the hill tops. Imperfect, sure, but ready to chase that wild horizon on two tired feet. This path, it's more than a walk; it's a chance to write my own story, one mile at a time. It's going to be a heck of a journey, bumps and all.

The Beach Huts at Barry

Penarth - Rhoose, January 13th 2023

Penarth waved goodbye as I set off just after sunrise. The clifftop walk, full of dog walkers' and their cheery "mornings" echoing in the mist. Soon Lavernock Point, where history hummed with the first radio signal across the open sea.

Today the sun peeked through the clouds, but the past week's rain had woven the fields into mini rivers. One treacherous step later, I found myself face-planting in the mud, executing a flawless (if unintended) demonstration of the classic belly flop. After confirming my audience consisted solely of bemused sheep, I heaved myself upright. Laughter at my own elegance replaced any grumbles as I trudged on, feeling less like a seasoned hiker and more like a toddler learning to navigate gravity.

Sully Islands, rocky guardians, watched as I passed Sully Sand and Bay, each name hints of pirate tales. Then came the road, a gauntlet of traffic and lorries, their spray-painting me with muddy rainbows. A flooded field mirrored the grey sky, but the path soon reappeared, a lifeline for weary walkers and cyclists.

Barry Docks burst into view, a modern surprise against the grey industry of days gone by. I couldn't resist Gavin and Stacey's stomping ground – Barry Island. Sun-kissed beach, crashing waves, the scent of fish and chips wafting through the air - a seaside postcard comes to life.

21   *The home of Gavin and Stacey*

Roman remains at Cold Knap Point gave way to the cool embrace of woodland, ending in Porthkerry Country Park. A final push, and there it was: Rhoose Point, the southernmost tip of Wales. I touched the stone monument, land meeting sea, south meeting west.

Job done. Boots muddy, muscles aching, cold, wet and happy. This path was turning me into an adventurer, one soggy field and salty spray at a time and I wouldn't trade it for anything.

Rhoose Point

Rhoose - Merthyr Mawr, January 20th 2023

Brrr, my nose practically froze solid as I stepped out of my sister's car. Bless her for being my chauffeur around South Wales particularly during this arctic blast! Rhoose it is, starting point of this coastal crusade. Limestone cliffs from Porthkerry, with remains of ancient fossils extend before me. It continues all the way to Ogmore, this butterscotch coloured wall protects the land against the dark sea that dashes the shore. Aberthaw Nature Reserve, once a lime works, now a haven for feathered friends – the decommissioned power station no longer drowns out their chirpy gossip.

Limpet Bay, nestled between the cliffs, promised adventure rather than a peaceful stroll. Llantwit Major, loomed in the distance. The cold must have befogged my brain because I swear I walked for hours without seeing another soul. Maybe that's why I launched myself across a mud puddle and over a stile. My flexibility went AWOL with the dinosaurs, so hoisting myself over was more of a pained grunt than a graceful leap. A kind young lady jogger snuck up on me (nearly gave me a heart attack!) and offered help, the embarrassment was enough to refind my flexibility and doing a full twisting double backflip, I dismounted the stile.

St. Donats, birthplace of the Rigid Inflatable Boat – talk about making a splash! Nash Point, with its lighthouse

The Glamorgan Heritage Coast

twins protecting the coast, became my next conquest. Clifftop views all the way – the beach would have been a better hike today but the coast path has other ideas. A stroll along Dunraven and the picturesque Heritage Coast, where the dazzling sun and sparkling sea converge, creating a resplendent vista that will captivate your senses. Ogmore by Sea, I pass a familiar looking face, local celebrity and Welsh Rugby Player, Gareth Thomas. By the time my walk weary brain had worked out who he was, it was too late. The sun sinking like a fiery ball, seemed the perfect end to the day. Except, sneaky disappearing underwater stepping stones, there was no way of crossing, so a walk upstream to a bridge, a field and a bouncy bridge finale. Perfect way to loosen the day's aches (and maybe some mud clinging to my boots).

What a day! Cold walk, sure, but an adventure etched in my bones. One fossil, one bird song, one near-drowning, and a bouncy bridge later. I'm one step closer to completing the Wales Coast Path.

27   *Trecco Bay Lookout Tower, Porthcawl*

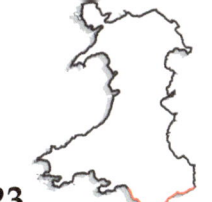

Merthyr Mawr - Aberavon, January 27th 2023

Another cold one, Merthyr Mawr in the morning is like biting into an ice cube! Big thanks to my sister for the drop-off but talk about a brainfart moment. Phone? Missing in action. Back we go, the car humming with laughter at my forgetfulness. An hour later, my phone clutched tighter than a winning lottery ticket, I'm finally off!

A quick road walk, then bam, Merthyr Mawr Nature Reserve. Europe's second largest sand dune, the Big Dipper, looms like a sleepy giant.

Around the bend, the path dipped, then broadened, revealing a vista that sent a ripple of pure joy through me. It wasn't just a beach; it was how I dreamt the walk would be. Sweet honey coloured sand, soft as icing sugar, shimmered under the low morning sun, spanning like a welcoming towel to the edge of the sea. In rhythmic sets, the playful yet forceful waves rolled toward shore, each crest whispering secrets to the shore in a language only my sun-warmed soul could understand. This was it, the reason I'd decided to walk this path, all that was missing was the flying fish jumping over the rainbow and a unicorn galloping along the beach. This would have been my dream. Each breath felt like a conscious choice, a deliberate filling of my lungs with pure beach air, chasing away the cobwebs and filling the hollow corners of my being with the essence of this coastal paradise. In that

Aberavon Beach

moment, adrift on a sea of sand and serenity, I understood why I'd signed up for this – not just for the escape, but for the rediscovery of a simpler rhythm, a deeper connection to the pulse of the earth and the song of the sea. On this beach, bathed in sunlight and embraced by the ocean's endless lullaby, I didn't just exist; I thrived.

Trecco Bay, Porthcawl – all names that roll off the tongue like a surfer's lullaby. Coney Amusement Park brings a burst of civilization – pavements, boardwalks, even prams and wheelchairs strolling on for miles in the sunshine. Kenfig Nature Reserve next, a green jewel behind the ochre sands.

Then reality bites. Margam Moors, a turn across some train tracks, then an industrial estate that wouldn't look out of place in a Batman movie. I get to the M4 and the Coast Path offers choices, I choose an urban adventure: it has to be quicker than a mountain walk, right?

So, it's grey and grimy streets all the way to Aberavon beachfront. Sun sinking low, casting long shadows, makes the contrast between grimy concrete and pristine sand even starker. But you know what? Even here, with the sea breeze swirling and the waves bellowing their welcome, I feel a smile grow across my face. Every step, every stumble, every detour – it's all part of the adventure. Next time, there's a whole new chuck of coastline waiting to be explored and I can see most of it from here.

The contrast between the beach and
the industry

Aberavon - Caswell, February 3rd 2023

Aberavon sand practically glitters under my feet, not the coal-dusted stuff of my childhood but clean and golden like a pirate's treasure. From here, today's walk extends around the coast to Mumbles and beyond, Mumbles Lighthouse a dot across the bay. Sun squints into my eyes, making me grin like a fool, wind whipping my hair into a seagull's nest. The air, salty and clean, filled my lungs like a healing elixir. This was raw beauty, unfiltered and exhilarating.

But a few steps later, the world spun on its axis. The gentle surf was replaced by the guttural growl of machinery, the scent of seaweed by the acrid tang of exhaust. Steel and concrete replaced the sun-kissed sand, the sky no longer a haven but a canvas smudged with smoke. It was a sensory assault, nature's delicate masterpiece crudely defaced by the harsh strokes of industry.

Passing Brunel Quay, over the old Briton Ferry Bridge. Below, the River Neath gurgles secrets to itself as traffic roars on the dual carriageways. I turn into a side road, canal shimmering beside me, along to Port Tennant. A left turn, docklands looming, and suddenly the city's heartbeat slows. River Tawe glistens like a mermaid's scales as I cross by the Swansea barrage. Then boom, the cycle track to Mumbles, heaven!

33   *Swansea Bay, looking at Mumbles*

Lifeboat stations, lighthouse, big red apple – Mumbles. Coast path beckons, smooth path, easy miles. Langland Bay with its iconic beach chalets, a picture of how life was in days gone by. Along the headland again, the final destination of the day Caswell. Dad scoops me up, I zip back to Aberavon to retrieve my car. Public transport wouldn't have been an option – it would've taken forever and left me way behind.

Caswell at sunrise

Caswell - Port Eynon, February 10th 2023

The headland was playing peek-a-boo with the sun, finally letting it creep over in a burst of shimmering silken light, tide lapping up like a happy puppy. Gorgeous light I got to admit, but with the tide in, it's road walking time, until I can escape onto the cliffs and get to Brandy Cove. Smugglers haven you say? Sounds more like a hangover cure to me.

Onwards to Pwlldu beach, a sneaky little bay tucked away from the crowds. Worth the walk mind you. Up I go, lungs wheezing like rusty bellows, and boom, Southgate – gateway to Three Cliffs. Now things get juicy. Ditch the main path, I have to see Pennard Castle. Ruins with a view, Sign me up! Back on track, hop-skip-and-jump over the stepping stones at Three Cliffs Bay, then tackle the sand dune monster. Legs screaming, come on, you can do it, shut up legs, why won't they stop? What a View! Forest interlude, cool and green, then BAM! Oxwich Burrows. Dunes again, taunting me with a perfectly good beach just a stone's throw away. Not cool Wales Coast Path, not cool. Past a fancy hotel and ancient church, then WHAM! Steps steeper than a politician's promises. Legs shaking like a flamingo on an iceberg, lungs begging for mercy.

On we go, past Oxwich Point, quiet as a library after closing time. Not even a seagull squawk. The Sands beach finally graced me with its presence, pretty enough to soothe the sand dune grudge. Plod, plod,

Three Cliff Bay

plod to Port Eynon, rain clouds rolling in like grumpy in-laws. Just as the drizzle turns into a downpour, Dad saves me by returning me to Caswell. To do this leg via public transport would be like wrestling an octopus for its roller skates. Not the smoothest walk Wales Coast Path, but you giveth good views and taketh away with sand dunes and steps from hell.

39   *Culver Hole*

Port Eynon - Llanmadoc, February 17th 2023

Fog so thick it could cut cake, wind trying to steal your eyebrows, and enough mud to fill a thousand wellies – that's the Gower on a fierce Friday. Starting at Port Eynon, I dredged through a caravan park, then climbed Port Eynon Point, like a wind-battered flag. Culver Hole told stories of pirates and treasures, leaving me content as I returned to the path and continued my day. Not many dare this Gower coast in fog and I get it. Black cows bigger than your nightmares, a bull worthy of its own horror movie – all looming out of the mist like fluffy phantoms. Then Mewslade Bay, a beach surprise! Surfers braving the weather, sand whispers drowned out by crashing waves. No photo-worthy Worm's Head today, sadly lost in the foggy soup.

Tourist conga lines from Worms Head to Rhossili village. A lane hiding behind the church, then to The Downs, where I slogged through a muddy track (the beach was RIGHT THERE!). Finally Llangennith and hello sand! Waves wrestling with fog. The whole beach swallowed in fog, like a stick inside a candy floss. Burry Holms, Llanmadog, and then Cwm Ivy - Scenic detour? In fog? Madness, right? The fog clung to Whitford Point like a ghostly veil, the lighthouse a fleeting silhouette—a mere hint of its presence. The shore was a pulse of waves upon shingle, while the estuary thrashed, a captive seeking its ocean escape. The incoming tide pushed back, a ceaseless dance between river and ocean – boom! Euphoria moment.

The Old Lifeboat Station at Rhossili

Best feeling of the whole walk so far. Back to Cwm Ivy, battered sea wall letting the wildlife party, and that is as much walking in the fog as I can handle for one day. Wild Gower, you may try to drown me in fog and mud but you also throw in moments of pure coastal magic. Bring on the sunshine next time though, okay?

Cwm Ivy Marsh

Llanmadoc - Bynea, 24th February 2023

It's the end of February (it's been feeling like rain-mageddon forever) and I score a sunny day for a change. My Sister drops me off and I head along the path, starting at Cwm Ivy Woods. You know that broken sea wall I saw the other day? Now I'm on the other side. The tide's high and it's swallowed the whole path. Guess plan A's out the window. I scramble through a field, down a cliff face steeper than my rent and finally rejoin the path along some marshy bit. Hoping the tide doesn't decide to play tag because there's nowhere to run!

Pass Weobley Castle, but it's hiding behind a jungle of overgrown bushes. Then comes this random stile chilling in a field, no fence or anything. Talk about weird walkin' sights. Just past Llanrhidian, I bump into these two walkers doing this "dip in every beach around Gower" thing (wild, I know). It turns out the road I'm on was underwater this morning but now it's a breeze with epic views. We saunter along till Crofty, then I'm back on solo mode.

Next up, a mix-up of pavements and a cycle track that continues for miles. Walking on a smooth track, easy mode, gotta love those quick-fleeting miles. The coast path isn't about comfort, nope. It throws up a steep hill, across a field, some long muddy track, then back on the road I just escaped, swerving around cars like a slalom skier. Finally after more twists and turns than a curly

45 *Somewhere on the North Gower coast,*
looking towards Weobley Castle

whirly, I find myself in a park near Loughor Castle (I have no idea how I got here!). Feeling like Alice in Wonderland, I cross Loughor Bridge (hello Carmarthenshire!) and reach the Blue Bridge where I call it a day. What a walk!

47   *One of the Shipwrecks along Cefn Siden*

Bynea - Kidwelly, March 3rd 2023

Crisp air, icy ground - perfect day for a walk, right? So I dragged my sister along as this is the flattest part of the Wales Coast Path. We set off from the blue bridge, crunching along a tarmac track past wetlands and golf courses. This part of the path overlaps the Heart of Wales Line Trail, part of a 141-mile monster walk but that's for another time.

Miles melted away as we followed the path, sneaking peeks at Llanelli docks and Sandy Water Park. Soon Burry Port popped up, where Amelia Earhart touched down after flying across the Atlantic. A charming lighthouse like a cherry Bakewell, a small step from the path and a break from the endless repetition of steps. Pembrey Country Park beckoned, but Wales' longest beach, Cefn Sidan, called louder. Shipwrecks, skeletons of boats from another time, their stories lost to the sea, littered the sand like forgotten toys. Past the beach and the weed-choked expanse of an old airstrip, we hit the road again, then meandered through a farm, a few fields of young lambs bleating their protest of our presence. The Kidwelly and Llanelli Canal became our final companion, taking us to the dock where we finally stopped. Not bad for a day's stroll, eh sis? Flat paths, fresh air, and a little taste of history.

The very Swollen River Towy

Kidwelly - Green Castle Woods, March 24th 2023

Cabin fever was kicking in after two weeks cooped up. Snow, then rain was forecast but didn't deliver, it stole my hiking mojo. Today's sunshine left me scrambling for excuses. "Nope!" I declared, boots already laced. Starting at Kidwelly, I abandoned the "pilgrimage" mentality. This was my journey and I'll decide my path.

Ignoring the official route I detoured to Kidwelly Castle (a stunner by the way) and took a quick photo. Just time for a swift hello, not another full exploration. Soon, I was whisked uphill, leaving the sea behind for the village of Llansaint. Inland it stayed, the promised ocean view a tease. Late March meant mud anyway, thanks to the "wettest ever" title this month was proudly wearing. Squelching through fields, dodging fertiliser spray, I descended into Ferryside. Bigger than expected, I marvelled at houses perched with envy-inducing views. Quiet lanes, fields, a cheeky woodland, and back to lanes I went. All this peacefulness was shattered by a large BOOM! That made me jump out of my skin. Just across the water at Pendine some military manoeuvres stole my zen like calm. Lane to road, road to busier road – yikes! Carmarthen awaited, its busy streets thrumming with the sounds of traffic and trains. Just past the footbridge, the promised path morphed into a shallow lake. With a sigh, I waded through, boots squishing. Beneath a

Carmarthens Bascule Bridge

skeletal bascule bridge, a relic of a navigable past, now the stagnant water choking the riverbed. From the frying pan into the fire, the lake-like path ends and I return to a road. This bit wasn't for the faint of heart. Cars whizzed by inches from my boots, a very uncomfortable stretch of road. I finally escaped the traffic chaos and find solace in Green Castle Woods, my endpoint. The day is over and my soggy boots stink. Now here's the question: do you chase adventure even when it chases you with a raincloud? Are the unexpected detours the most interesting parts of the journey?

53 *Llanstephan Beach with it's Castle*

Green Castle Woods - St Clears, March 31st 2023

From Green Castle Woods, I plunged back onto the Wales Coast Path, it's still March, and it's still soggy underfoot. Today's adventure: a soggy loop from Carmarthen to St Clears. Farm tracks, flooded fields, and paths straight from yesteryear, with drovers as my invisible companions. Llanstephan appeared ahead, its radiant beach cradled by a sky-high castle.

Scott's Bay stole my breath – endless sand, open sky, pure freedom. Then, a farm track, a lost path, and back on track. Across the Taf, Laugharne winked across the water. Three farm dogs greeted me – two fluffy Jack Russells, practically tripping over themselves in their excitement and a wise old sheepdog, holding back with a watchful stare. Suddenly, the older Jack transformed. A growl rumbled in his throat as he lunged, teeth tearing into my flesh above my knee. The shock of pain was quickly overtaken by rage. No owner in sight, just me and three dogs. Could I even continue my walk? What if it was more than just a nip? My heart thumped in my ears as I took a cautious step back. The dogs ran off and I made my escape, I hobbled along as the path turned into a marsh, sucking my boots and testing my sanity. Soaked and grumpy, I found refuge in a woodland, checked my wound. To my relief it was just a scratch, I left the woodland only to face flooded country roads again. Path signs mocked me, pointing into fields transformed into giant lakes. No way! I'm

55   *The flooded road*

sticking to the road, I braved the dual carriageway, dodging cars and their angry spray. Finally, St. Clears, the end of a soggy, dog-bitten adventure. Not the prettiest walk, but the grit in my boots and the sting on my leg. Those were badges of a wild, watery Welsh wander.

Laugharne Castle

St Clears - Wisemans Bridge, April 2nd 2023

Palm Sunday, morning sunshine, church bells tolling and the open road beckoned. Ditching the usual midweek routine, I set off from St Clears for another coastal adventure. Traffic dodged, thanks to a hidden path just off the road, until...THUD! A treacherous boardwalk over a swamp sent me sprawling, landing squarely on my ribs. Ouch!

Bruised but not broken, I pressed on, fields and lanes giving way to familiar sights – Laugharne, Dylan Thomas' stomping ground. The boat house, the castle, rings of his poetic spirit filling the air. Lush Laugharne, lapped by the luminous sea, lies where the lazy Taf tickles the tide.

Then a detour. Armed with a tip to bypass the MOD area and stroll Pendine Sands in its entirety, I followed cryptic directions. Only to find myself staring at a "Danger, No Entry, Debris may Explode" sign, an hour of precious time sacrificed.

Back on track, the road section, supposedly soul-crushing, turned out pleasant enough. The tourist hordes at Pendine? Not my cup of tea. Time to escape the crowds.

Up a gruelling cliff with steps I clambered, gasping for air with every step. The reward was sweet – solitude and an impressive panorama of the beach below. The path snaked along the cliff face, offering glimpses of a

Marros Sands

time-worn treasure – Marros Sands, a secluded beauty accessible only to the determined few.

Erosion forced a detour, sending me down to the road and into Amroth, another tourist magnet. passing the Smugglers Arms, the busy beer garden taunted me but I stayed strong. Tourist, tourist, everywhere! Up the hill I trekked, through a shady woodland, finally dropping into Wisemans Bridge, where my chariot awaited.

Tenby Harbour

Wisemans Bridge - Freshwater East, April 14th 2023

The Pembrokeshire part of the Wales Coast Path sings to the soul and today, I was answering its siren call. Starting at Wisemans Bridge, through a few pedestrian tunnels, there was Saundersfoot. A quick stomp through, the harbour was under maintenance, so on I plunged into the emerald embrace of a woodland, boots sinking into the rain-soaked mud. Poles, usually mere baggage, became trusty companions as I clambered up the slippery slopes.

Emerging from the trees, Tenby's candy-coloured houses burst into view, a vibrant counterpoint to the rugged cliffs. The tourist crowds washed around the town, but the path wisely skirted the edges, offering glimpses of the seaside bustle without getting caught in the current.

South Beach flowed out like an ivory ribbon, inviting me down for a barefoot stroll. Gitar Point rewarded me with panoramic views of Caldey Island, a smudge of green in the sapphire sea. Just as I rounded the bend, the heavens opened, unleashing a hailstorm that battered and blew me about the clifftop.

Lydstep Cove, nestled snugly in its bay, offered a brief respite. Gentle waves lapped the shingle beach, a lullaby to the storm's fury. The path, a relentless rollercoaster, soon had me climbing Lydstep Point,

Church Doors Cove

then plunging into another inlet, only to ascend again.

Church Doors Cove, framed by dramatic cliffs and accessed by a vertiginous staircase, stole my breath with its raw beauty. Back up the steps (legs issuing me a formal protest!), I skirted the MOD base, catching tantalising glimpses of another hidden beach gem. Manorbier, with its soft satin sands and imposing King's Quoit burial chamber, was next on the menu. Then came the daintily named Swanlake Bay, where I finally snagged a break, trying to dry off with the waves rolling and tumbling up the beach.

Freshwater East, a crescent of pristine sand backed by dunes, was the perfect finale. This, I thought, is how beaches were meant to be. As the sun dipped towards the horizon, painting the sky in fiery hues, I knew I'd found my happy place.

Pembrokeshire's coast path may have thrown mud, rain, and hail at me, but it also lavished me with ravishing beauty, hidden coves, and the soul-stirring rhythm of the sea. That, my friends, is a trade I'll gladly make any day.

St.Govan's Chaple

Freshwater East - Freshwater West, April 21st 2023

Sunshine and blue skies were my reward for returning for another section of the Pembrokeshire leg of the Wales Coast Path. Up the steps from Freshwater East, Trewent Point unfolded like a postcard, revealing the epic beach in all its glory. Soon, rock faces striped like Skye's Kilt Rock surprised me, nature's own tartan. Stackpole Quay charmed me with its harbour and a dramatic fault line, and in the ethereal hush of the early morning, as the golden rays of dawn gracefully touched the world, casting a warm embrace upon the ocean. Barafundle Bay unveiled itself as the star of the show. A shore of untouched and empty sand laid before my eyes, a serene and tranquil reward for my early start. The soft caress of the gentle breeze carried the hushed sound of waves, lapping at the shore, creating a symphony that was both calming and invigorating. It was a moment of pure bliss, a snapshot of nature's beauty. I'd like to stay here forever but no rest for the wicked. Broadhaven was next, then I couldn't resist a detour – I took a stroll around Bosherston Lily Ponds – I was early for the lilies but who can say no to feeding wild birds straight out of your hand? A swift lap of the ponds, then it was all about tearing through the dunes and getting cosy with the cliffs until I hit St Govan's Chapel. This amazing little place tucked right into the rocks. Count the steps down and count them back up, you'll never have the same number. Be warned, the military lays claim to the

The Green Bridge of Wales

next magnificent section, forcing a detour inland. It's fields, cows and a lonely viewing tower, a stark contrast to the dramatic coastline I'm missing. Cars became my unwelcome companions on the final piece to Freshwater West, twilight chasing me on the road. This day was over but that forbidden beauty behind Castlemartin haunted me – I had to return.

Three weeks after my first attempt, I went back for round two, this time with a solid late-day sprint. Passed St Govan's and the coast just showed off: Bullslaughter Bay was all shades of blue, the Witches' Cauldron was swirling with mystery and sea birds made a cackling noise, Elegug Stacks stood tall, and then there it was – the Green Bridge of Wales, just epic. It took me three tries to get here but it was worth it! The most vibrant bloom in a field full of wildflowers.

Freshwater West

Freshwater West - Pembroke, April 28th 2023

A week later, I craved the raw power of Freshwater West. The wind howled, mist swirled and waves crashed – surfer's paradise, not for the faint of heart. I devoured the beach's wildness, then vanished into the fog, clinging to the cliff path as a strange hum buzzed in my ears. Visibility sucked and the wind threatened to yank me skyward. Miles later, the culprit of the buzzing revealed itself: a monstrous radio mast, shouting it's messages to the sky. This part was different – emptier, wilder. West Angle Bay welcomed me with sand-blasted eyes (no wonder camels have those lashes!) and onward I trekked past the lifeboat station and into Angle village. A tarmac path, Jersey cows in emerald fields, then back to tarmac – civilization intruding in the form of a power station. Even industry couldn't erase the beauty – the smell of the wild garlic, the ducks quacking as they preen themselves, thick lichen painting the trees a vibrant green, proof of the surprisingly clean air.

Up a lane, down a farm track and then...chaos. A bovine stampede, a tangle of horns and hooves, waiting at a gate. A herd of dairy cows, desperate to be milked. Panic clawed at my throat. They wouldn't leave, they wouldn't yield. Back to the track, heart hammering, only to find myself face-to-face with another herd, a hulking bull at its head.

Fate, it seemed, had other plans. A gap, fleeting and

71   *Under a jetty in the Milford Haven Waterway*

precious, opened in the cow wall. I lunged, legs pumping, adrenaline, a fiery cocktail in my veins. The gate, rusty and creaking, swung open, offering sanctuary. I scrambled through, stumbled down a few steps and ended up sprawled out on the path, my chest heaving, lungs burning. Relieved to be out of the field, relieved to be safe. A road walk into Pembroke, I'd rather dodge the cars than be chased by the cows.

Pembroke's tarmac streets never looked so welcoming. Legs wobbly, spirit exhilarated, I called it a day. Cows, cliffs, and a touch of industrial grit.

Pembroke Castle

Pembroke - Sandy Haven, May 5th 2023

A week wiser and my boots seasoned, I returned to Pembroke and tackled the coast path with renewed swagger. Castle moat overthrown, I plunged into woodland and fields, blindly trusting the Pembrokeshire signs. Random streets gave way to a misty vista of the Neyland Bridge, the estuary shimmering like a mirage. Down I went, deeper into the damp embrace of fog and streets, until suddenly, I was swallowed by the ironness of the Neyland Bridge. The wind was so fierce it felt like it was tossing me around like a stray leaf, slamming me across the pavement and back to the railings. Shelter, where art thou? Finally, the opposite shore offered refuge. Road walking, marina crossing, then a near miss with a wrong turn – thankfully, woods offered a brief respite. Neyland, new territory, unfolded before me, murmurs of its dockyard past and Brunel's legacy clinging to the air.

The road turned to industrial sprawl, the chill of this sterile metal world, a curious dance of oil refinery, fields, and cage bridges. Shipping beacons stood with watchful eyes, guiding me towards Milford Haven, an unspoiled beauty with a quiet promenade and harbour, its streets a charming maze. Through Gelliswick Bay, its lone pebble beach hinting at touristy dreams, I navigated the industrial symphony of cranes and ships.

Kilroom

Then, turning a corner, the Milford Haven Waterway loosened its grip on my spirit. Kilroom Beach, a slither of sand against the steel giants, washed away the tension. By the time Sandy Haven shimmered into view, I was pure zen. Timing my friends is everything. Low tide revealed the stepping stones, a final challenge, I skipped across just as the tide turned, claiming its watery victory. Day done, boots triumphant, spirit soaring. Pembrokeshire, you never cease to surprise.

77 *Rook's Nest Point*

Sandy Haven - Martins Haven, May 12th 2023

Gone are the days of dodging puddles and battling wind – May has painted Pembrokeshire a vibrant canvas of blue skies and endless sunshine. Sandy Haven's stepping stones, now submerged, hiding from a week ago. Today, spring was my companion, Bees buzzed and butterflies fluttered as I skipped along the coast path.

Monks Haven, with its intriguing ruin and random beach wall, was a quick hello before Dale, a haven for water sports, came into view. A split in the path – high tide, low tide? Feeling confident under the sun's warm gaze, I gambled on the low route. A broken boardwalk bridge loomed, a "cross at low tide" sign offering a playful challenge. A fisherman's booming encouragement echoed as I leaped across the gap, landing with a splash and earning a hearty laugh. Souvenir: wet socks. I took a quick break to squeeze the water out of my socks, a small reward for conquering the boardwalk. Just then, a flicker of green amidst the shells - a frosted piece of sea glass, tumbled smooth by the sea. It joined me on my adventure, a reminder of the day's triumphs and wet socks.

Dale pulsed with life but I yearned for quiet tracks. Fields baked under the sun, cows napping in blissful indifference. Soon, St. Ann's Head rose, its lighthouse standing as a vigilant guardian. Geology took centre

Saint Ann's Head Lighthouse

stage – rich red rock, banded like a masterpiece, while pink flowers swayed in the breeze. This was spring in all its glory!

Westdale Bay, a local secret with crashing waves, unfolded before me, this beauty was mine to discover. Passing a forgotten airfield, a testament to the area's military history, I arrived at Marloes Sands. Photographers captured its magic, the copper expanse and dramatic rock formations, showing how the earth was created . Even Gateholm Island, silhouetted against the azure sky, couldn't compete with this precious find.

Boots feeling heavy with wanderlust, I continued my journey to Martins Haven, I'm parched like you wouldn't believe. As the day neared its end, the allure of Skomer Island was irresistible. I had to see the island of puffins, no boat! I make the trek up to the headland. A final clamber revealed its rugged, bird-filled form, a visit for another time.

81   *A marker stone, with Stack Rocks lost at sea*

Martins Haven - Newgale, May 19th 2023

So, another week, another chunk of Welsh Coast Path to tame! Starting in Martins Haven, I traded the trusty red sandstone cliffs for something more... earthy. Snakes? Great, thanks for the heads-up, sign. Not exactly calming as I swished my way through the overgrown path. At least Stack Rocks with a disappearing hole in it took my focus for much of the day.

There I was, strolling along the path, feeling all rugged and outdoorsy. Then, WHAM! A blur of brown darts across my path, there was a high-pitched shriek that even Katherine Jenkins couldn't hit. My heart pumped a few extra beats as I envisioned fangs, scales and the unmistakable slither of... a field mouse. Yep, that's right folks, nature's version of popcorn was the source of my operatic outburst. The little guy probably thought I was auditioning for a Go.Compare advert, because he shot off like a furry rocket, leaving me red-faced and questioning my own bravery (or lack thereof). So much for conquering the wilderness; apparently, even pint-sized rodents can leave me quivering in my hiking boots. Who knows, maybe that mouse will tell his grandkids about the terrifying human who screamed like a banshee.

After that minor meltdown, I chilled on Little Haven Beach, mesmerised by the swirly rock patterns (geology rocks!). Druidston Haven was next, a cute

Newgale Sands

beach with a waterfall but I'll be honest, those cliffs were a tad too close for comfort. Feeling more open-minded (and less claustrophobic), I strolled onward to Nolton Haven - another haven on the haven list! Finally, Newgale Sands spread out before me, a haven for surfers and campers. With that, my day (and leg muscles) were done!

Dinas Fach

Newgale - Whitesands, June 2nd 2023

A symphony of rustling campers and their breakfast shenanigans welcomed me back to Newgale after my injury hiatus. Armed with my trusty bone-conducting headphones, I set off on the trail, ready for a musical adventure. Now, these headphones are amazing – they let you jam out to your tunes while still being in tune with the world around you. It's like having a personal DJ without missing a single moo or baa from the fields I was strolling through.

Speaking of fields, let's just say the electric fence separating me from a herd of curious cows was a welcome sight. No bovine close encounters today, thank you very much. The path led me to the cliff edge, revealing Solva Harbour nestled in its own little cove, looking like a secret hideaway. It was all charm and quaintness, but soon the scenery amped up the drama with towering cliffs, mysterious caves, and even a few rogue islands here and there. This coastline was like a treasure hunt, with bustling beaches, hidden chapels, and secluded harbours – each with its own tale to tell.

The sun decided to join the party, turning my cheeks a delightful shade of pink. I reached Pen Dal-aderyn, the most westerly point of mainland Wales, expecting some grand monument or something. Nope, just breathtaking views of Ramsey Island. Onwards I marched, avoiding the eternal roar of the wind at St. Justinians lifeboat station. Seriously, nature's breath

87 *RNLI St Davids Lifeboat Station*

was so strong I could barely keep my eyes open. No pain, no gain, right? Because then, Whitesands Beach appeared like a mirage, promising the ultimate reward: ICE CREAM!

With tired legs but a happy heart (and a face that looked like a tomato, except for the two perfectly white circles where my headphones had been – talk about a tan line fail!), I soaked in the last bit of coastal magic before calling it a day. The verdict? Bone-conducting headphones: 10/10. Untanned headphone circles: not so much. But hey, who needs a perfect tan when you've got the sounds of the sea and a belly full of ice cream?

Blue Lagoon- Abereiddi

Whitesands - Strumble Head, June 9th 2023

Sun scorching my back, I crunched along the Pembrokeshire coast. Spectacular views, sure but who knew "record-breaking heat" meant feeling like an overbaked crisp? It all started nicely - waves hushing up the beach, birds singing and wildflowers bobbing in the morning breeze. At first my trusty map app worked ... then KAPUT! No signal, no map, just me and confusing waymarkers.

I found Abereiddy Bay, it shimmered like a mirage, its cobalt waters and cliff-jumping crew, jumping 30 feet into ice cold water, utter madness. Hold on, where were the ice cream vans, the burger stalls? My thirst, a mumble at first, became a persistent call. Finally, the map app flickered back to life. Great, what else could go wrong today?

Porthgain offered history, not hydration. Slate scars tell tales of industry, the ruined Trefin Mill stories of lives gone by. Each cove, a fresh hope for a shop, a cafe, anything with a liquid soul. Porth this, Porth that, a dry cove after another.

Tiny Abercastle, nestled in a cove with its grand burial chamber, seemed promising, but nada. By Abermawr and Aberbach, the sun cast long shadows, my tongue sandpaper-rough. Three villages, countless coves, not a single sip.

91 *Pwllcrochan*

Pwllcrochan's geology lesson, with its mind-bending rocks, did little for my drought. My brow caked in salt where earlier sweat had been, each step a protest. Pwll Deri, Porth Mae Melyn, the names blurred past like silent film. Dusk arrived, moths joined the party. Then, salvation! Strumble Head Lighthouse, its light blinking as the sunset. Half an hour, that's all it took. I practically ran, fueled by the promise of water. Reaching my car, two litres disappeared faster than a magician's rabbit.

Day done, right? Wrong. My journey home was extended by an hour due to roads being closed. Just another twist in this parched, Pembrokeshire adventure.

Cwm-yr-Eglwys

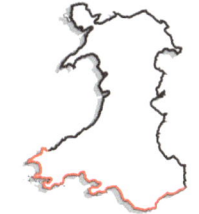

Strumble Head - Newport, June 16th 2023

One week after my epic thirst-fest, I was back. I have to change the way I tackle this path, as walking over 20 miles on a hot sunny day is pure madness. My plan involves a tent, fueled by a hopeful spirit (alright, perhaps a bit over-optimistic). Sunshine was forecast, so two days of hiking and a starry night awaited!

Strumble Head's lighthouse and cliff top views greeted me, then onto Fishguard's groaning ferry (so loud, even gulls flee). From the old harbour's salty charm and a castle echoing with battles, I wandered into a caravan park maze. Lost again (let's not judge!) and finding a craving for ice cream, I emerged onto the dark sands of Dinas Head, a pirate's island rising from the sea. Past the dramatic headland, Cwm-yr-Eglwys delivered my dream - ice cream by a ruined church, waves gently lapping the shore.

Parrog and Newport were next, the tide was in! Water lapped at the house walls. A Busy place on a Friday evening, I found my campsite and put my tent up. It's been many years since I last camped, I'm not sure what I'm supposed to do. I settle down for the night in the dark, flappy noisy tent. Then, rain! Weeks of sunshine, no rain forecast, but my first camping trip became a washout.

Careg Coetan

Newport - Cardigan, June 17th 2023

Newport to Cardigan by car, the bus whizzed me back to Newport. Careg Coetan, an ancient burial chamber standing through time, was worth the detour. Rain stopped just as I left, emerald hills glowing across the sun-warmed estuary.

Then, things got epic. The path clung to the cliff, with a sharp ascent, lungs wheezing like manic bagpipes. Wow, the views! Pwll y Wrach's turquoise pool, Ceibwr Bay's dancing rocks, banded like fresh cut grass - These are the moments that suck the air out of you.. .and leave you searching for an inhaler, leaving me in awe of nature's grand landscaping.

Reaching Cemaes Head, a sign read "Pembrokeshire Coast Path - First Gate." A moment of realisation. I was walking the whole thing... backwards! Not the plan, but okay, who says you can't walk a trail in reverse?

On I went, dodging cars and admiring Saint Dogmaels, an ancient monastery echoing with stories of old. Just like that, Pembrokeshire was done, hello Ceredigion! I had a little more to walk, the path stays on the road most of the way into Cardigan, but it did try to send me into a field of cows. I stood by the gate for a second, trying to judge their response. The whole herd ran to the gate, they had huge horns, that was enough for me. I retreated to the road and refused to leave its safety. A happy ending in Cardigan.

Mwnt

Cardigan - Aberporth, June 23rd 2023

I'm on another two-day hike, starting from Cardigan. The weather is gloomy and wet. I walk through fields and roads until I reach Gwbert, where the rain gets heavier. I feel miserable.

On my way out of Gwbert, I met an ambitious walker. He tells me he's walking from John o' Groats to Land's End and adding a loop around Wales. He also tells me, my next two days are the hardest of his trip, even lumpier than Scotland. I wonder why I'm doing this.

As I journey along the path, the view of Cardigan Island unfolds, a prelude to the splendour ahead. Then, Mwnt reveals itself—an exquisite haven where straw coloured sands meet the embrace of azure waters. It's a place that offers more than just natural beauty; it's equipped with all the conveniences: well-maintained toilets, ample parking and a selection of snacks to savour.

The true marvel of Mwnt? The dolphins! There, in the crystalline waves, they dance, an enchanting sight that captivates and delights. I stand there, transfixed, as these graceful creatures perform their aquatic ballet. This moment, this place—it's the pinnacle of my journey, a memory etched in joy and wonder. This is the reason for this walk.

I have to move on, past the chapel and along the path. I pass through more fields and an MOD base. I finally reach Aberporth, my destination. I find my campsite and settle in for another night of showers. I should have a TV show about predicting the weather and walks around Wales.

Tresaith

Aberporth - Newquay, June 24th 2023

Sunshine beat down on Aberporth as I started the next day. Gone were the drizzly blues, replaced by the sizzle of the hottest June on record. Swimmers splashed in the sea, they were swimming out into the blue and along the coast, I passed quirky train-carriage homes.

At Tresaith, a waterfall cascaded onto the beach, a sight almost stolen by the group of speedy swimmers who somehow arrived before me despite my brisk pace.

The climb up the mountain track was a lung buster, but the reward was a glimpse of Penbryn: halfway point of the Wales Coast Path! I celebrated with a well-deserved feast at the National Trust cafe – coffee, cake, sandwich, and a huge grin. Time for more breaks, I decided.

Back to the hills, up and down like a yo-yo. Llangrannog bustled with tourists, a stark contrast to the quiet "secret beach" of Cwmtydu, a well-kept secret that locals have intently protected. Finally, after miles of sun-baked fields, I reached Newquay. Feet throbbing but my heart soared. Another day ticked off, another step closer to the journey's end.

Aberaeron

Newquay - Llanrhystud, July 7th 2023

My final two day hike! Newquay basking in sunshine, sea sparkling blue. I battled past the tourist crowds (even early in the morning!), wandered through the village and hit the beach. The tide was in, the path was out. Fenced-hopped, scrambled up eroded steps, landed in a caravan park (oops!). I found the escape route, rejoined the path (phew!).

Newquay marked the end of the lumpy roller-coaster of cliffs, so today was chill: woods, fields, valleys, holiday villages. Boom, Aberaeron appeared. Multicoloured pastel houses, oozing character. Everyone I mention it to loves it, no wonder! Refuelled with food and harbour-watching, I pressed on. Aberarth was a quick hop, the path lingering through its streets. Coastline return, fields galore, then Llanon. The path detoured inland, the busy coast road, the village roads, a quiet church visit, then spat me back into the wild. Cow field after cow field (where are the Welsh sheep?!). Finally Llanrhystud, the end of day. Time for a well-earned rest!

The Cliffs of Cardigan Bay

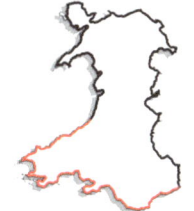

Llanrhystud - Aberystwyth, July 8th 2023

Another day, another early start. A storm is coming, I must hurry to Aberystwyth before the rain pounds and pushes me off the mountains. Out of Llanrhystud, up a hill with dazzling views of Cardigan Bay. Rain clouds loom to the south. Yep, caught a downpour soon after. Jacket on, then off, then on again - equally wet either way! But hey, this solo section was bliss. Just me, the path and the occasional refreshing shower.

Aberystwyth finally emerged, a welcome sight nestled beneath a steep hill. I made it before the real storm hit and couldn't have been happier to call it quits. Some days not a lot happens and that's okay. Homeward bound! This coast path isn't always sunshine and rainbows.

Sarn Gynfelyn

Aberystwyth - Borth, July 14th 2023

Borth blunder! I missed the train by a whisker and watched it chug away as I reached the station. An hour later, I finally set off to Aberystwyth, battling a tourist multitude before finding solace on the coast path. A quick jaunt along the prom and a kick of 'The Bar' for luck before starting up Constitution Hill (staggering view!), then...rain clouds looming.

Wind at my back acted as a sail, I zoomed past Clarach Bay, holiday park and Sarn Cynfelyn, a shingle spit to the lost land under Cardigan Bay. Borth beach called, but coastal erosion forced a detour. Snack in hand, I strolled the "straightest street in Wales," where the paths diverged. The Wales Coast Path took a right, but I went straight to finish the Ceredigion Coast Path. Petrified tree stumps at Ynyslas at low tide and the Dovey Estuary's majesty awaited! With a view across the water to Aberdovey, just a mile or so away, but it would take me 2 days to get there. Not a bad start to a big week of walking, despite the train fumble. Onwards!

The green rolling hills

Borth - Machynlleth, July 15th 2023

Ditching the sea today, I marched onward along the Wales Coast Path. No ocean views but Borth Bog, a giant peat bog made up for it with a butterfly ballet under the morning sun. After a delicious breakfast in Tre'r-ddol, I plunged into the woods, only to emerge into a field with a jaw-dropping panorama of the Dovey Estuary. Then a rain shower rolled in, turning the scene dramatic. The storm descended with a roar, obliterating the gentle landscape. The relentless thunder pounded my eardrums and the lightning painted monstrous, fleeting shapes on my eyelids. My phone flickered a pathetic beacon in the darkness, unusable with the amount of water pouring down its screen. I was cut off, alone, surrounded by the desperate bleating of sheep, whose usual hiding spots offered no sanctuary. Escape meant plunging into a raging river that had swallowed the path, each step sending icy water surging through my socks.

On exposed mountains, the rain continued, minus the light show. Winding through woods, fields, and lanes, I eventually dried off under a sky finally showing mercy. I hoped to see an Osprey around here but only got treated to a mysterious bird call. A mile of road walking followed, a blessing considering the puddle-infested ground. Finally, Machynlleth's rooftops peeked over a hill and I practically skipped down to town.

111   *Where's the path gone?*

Victory is mine! – the daily walk is done. My campsite awaits but the weather has other plans. My valiant attempt at pitching a tent was a comedy of errors, so I surrendered and slept soundly in the car. Not the best ending to a day but at least I was dry and able to continue tomorrow.

Aberdovey Beach

Machynlleth - Tywyn, July 16th 2023

Back in Machynlleth, grey skies loomed but at least it wasn't raining! Time to leave the town and head for the coast. Dodging traffic cones (thanks, roadworks!), I reached Dovey Bridge. This bridge was why I'd spent the day walking inland yesterday and meant today no coast vibes till later. The water raged high, barely leaving the bridge arches visible. A quick sprint across (splash-free) took me to the other side, followed by a quick stroll and then up a steep hill. Welcome to Snowdonia, my second National Park conquest!

Forest paths and forestry roads led me to Pennal and a charming holiday village. After navigating a woodland path and a field (with a slight wrong turn thanks to sneaky signage), I braved a lane, a field, and a herd of cows whose resident bull sent me shivers with his glare. Back up the mountain, the sun finally graced me with its presence, revealing extraordinary views of the Dovey Estuary and Borth (where I was just two days ago!). Following the path, I descended through fields and woodlands, finally arriving in Aberdyfi.

Picture this: a marvellous seaside town bursting with character. I strolled along the road, then onto the beach – my first proper beach walk since Newquay's tide-cut mission. This beach was paradise: dry, windswept and adorned with a gentle mist. Shells and jellyfish littered the 3 glorious miles and I loved every second of it.

Tywyn Beach

Near Tywyn, a bird spotted! It resembled a seagull but with a striking black and white mask. Surely this was an Osprey? Experts crushed my dreams, insisting it wasn't. Still, Tywyn marked the end of my day's journey, and what a journey it was! This unexplored corner of Wales had me smitten. Sure, I might have gotten lost, dodged angry bulls and faced an imposter osprey, but that's all part of the adventure, right? Who needs an osprey sighting when you have 3 miles of wondrous beach to yourself?

Stiles like these only start as I entered Snowdonia

Tywyn - Fairbourne, July 17th 2023

Tywyn was winning me over! This seaside town, a breath of fresh air with its train link to the Midlands. If I lived around Birmingham this would be a perfect weekend getaway. Bright and early, I left via the caravan park, sunshine warming my back as I walked along a quiet road. Suddenly, the path plunged into a field of tall grass, the heat sapping my energy as I felt myself slowly climbing. Reaching a sheep-filled field, the path flattened out, revealing a panorama that stopped me dead in my tracks. It was the most extraordinary view I'd seen yet! From Barmouth on the lower right, the coast spanned in a giant arc to Porthmadog and down the Llyn Peninsula. For the first time I saw the vastness of my upcoming journey and it looked… intimidating.

Continuing on, I stumbled upon a strange structure in a field. As luck would have it, the farmer tending his sheep was happy to chat. It turns out, it wasn't a burial chamber, as I thought but a wolf trap! He generously pointed out coastal highlights, his excitement matching my own for the view. Grateful for the information, I toodled along, only to be stumped by a damaged signpost. Misinterpreting its direction, I followed yellow markers for miles, ending up in a seemingly dead-end field.

Panic rising, I whipped out my map. That signpost had led me astray, onto a different long-distance trail with

Fairbourne

similar markings. Spotting the real coast path in the distance, I retraced my steps, frustration churning in my stomach. When I finally reached Llwyngwril, I was two hours behind schedule.

Faced with dwindling daylight and a gloomy forecast for the rest of the week, I made a tough call: abandon the coastal path. It climbed high into the hills, a risky adventure with approaching darkness. Defeated, I trudged up the road, enjoying the beach view as I entered Fairbourne. My first failed day – a harsh reality check. One 20-mile day a week was easy, but these consecutive walks were taking their toll. The wrong turn hadn't helped, even seasoned walkers get lost sometimes. Who knows, maybe tomorrow will be a better day.

Morfa Dyffryn

Fairbourne - Harlech, July 18th 2023

Grey clouds replaced the sunshine in Fairbourne, but at least it wasn't raining yet. I strolled along the promenade, checking out the WWII dragon's teeth – tank stoppers with more history than bite. A group of teenagers trudged past in the opposite direction, their "Duke of Edinburgh Award" enthusiasm a distant memory (poor kids).

Crossing Barmouth Bridge was an adventure – construction zones, workers and their noise everywhere. Luckily, I squeezed through before they closed it (that would've meant a 12-mile detour!). I'm standing on this bridge and the view's a killer – the town, the mountains and the water's so still it's like a mirror. Then I found the toll booth on the Barmouth side, it asked for cash. Who carries cash these days? I'm digging through my pockets and out pops the piece of sea glass from Dale – no way I'm parting with that. It's like the crown jewel of my trip. So I quickly swap it for some spare change and keep it moving. Barmouth felt like a sleepy amusement park, waiting to wake up after 10am. Along the beachfront, high tide roared. Waves pummelling the seawall, showering unsuspecting passersby. Ditching the soaked scenery, I joined the road – pavement, my hero!

Then, the drizzle started. Ugh, drizzle. Give me a downpour any day. A milestone gleamed: "Harlech 7 miles." Perfect, a leisurely 2-hour walk, I'll be done by

Harlech Castle

lunch. But the coast path had other plans. Stone-walled fields became a maze, their endless passages testing my navigation skills. (Who likes walking inside field rooms?) Rejoining the road, I reached Morfa Dyffryn beach. Drizzling, windy, but strangely charming. A sign made me chuckle: "Warning, naturist swimming or sunbathing." In this weather? No worries there! Just me and the seabirds for miles. Reaching Shell Island, my plans took an unexpected turn. I longed to see Harlech Castle, so I abandoned the path in favour of a sensible cycle track and viewpoint. Airfield, woodland, bridge, harbour, church – with each step the rain faded. Climbing a hill, a creature resembling a ferret darted across the road – a first for me! Down steep steps later, I crossed the railway and hit Harlech Beach. Two beach walks in one day? Spoiling me coast path! The sand glistened with strands of auburn, whitecaps sparkled on crashing waves, a stark contrast to the grey, gloomy sky. Harlech welcomed me with open arms, ending my day on a high note, despite the weather's best efforts.

Portmeirion

Harlech - Porthmadog, July 19th 2023

Another day, another punishing walk! Leaving Harlech's domineering castle behind, I snapped another photo (just in case). Soon, I was stomping through wet, thigh-high grass, hoping the ground wasn't hiding a swampy surprise. The reward was a captivating view of Portmeirion's colourful houses across the water, spreading out like a playful paint splatter.

The road led me alongside the train tracks, where a majestic steam train puffed into Penrhyndeudraeth station. Feeling smug about the dry weather, I marched past the Snowdonia National Park HQ, the Portmeirion turnoff... wait, wasn't I supposed to turn there? Panic set in - there was no coast path marker!

Backtracking and double-checking, I plunged into a field, following a marker that led me to... a dead end. Talk about frustrating! I returned to the marker and turned right before it (a first) and found myself on the Portmeirion entrance lane. My GPS was acting wonky but I knew something was off. Asking for help, I learned I wasn't alone - many get lost here. The "path" I found had zero coast path markers. How did I even end up at Boston Lodge, a train halt for the Blaenau Ffestiniog steam train? I couldn't take credit for my navigation skills today.

127   *The Steam Train at Porthmadog*

Reaching the Porthmadog sea wall marked the end of my journey. It was a glamorous finish, I had one heck of a confusing adventure, at least I wasn't stuck in a swamp! Sometimes, even seasoned walkers get turned around, but the key is to ask for help and laugh it off. Even getting lost can be part of the fun (especially when you end up near a cool steam train!).

Morfa Bychan

Porthmadog - Pwllheli, July 20th 2023

Porthmadog slept before the tourist crowds and I set off, leaving the harbour for the quiet and cute Borth y Gest. The peaceful world greeted me with a mirror-calm estuary, a lone paddleboarder the only ripple on its surface. Even through Pen y Banc Nature Reserve, the quiet held, offering pure beauty and tranquillity. Ah, bliss!

But serenity ended abruptly at Morfa Bychan Headland. The dramatic draft was back, cars dotted the beach – civilization reclaimed me. Criccieth welcomed me with its imposing castle and a delicious breakfast. Refreshed, I strolled past the castle, the gentle waves lapping the shingle beach with a soothing rhythm. Then, two miles of road walking – a quick way to melt the miles! Back to the coast, a sign warning of snakes (yikes!) preceded a holiday park and a headland. Finally, a glorious 3-mile beach walk at sunset, leading me to Pwllheli. Not the most dramatic day, but a perfect balance of accord and advancement, ending with a seaside sunset. Sometimes, simple beauty is the best reward. Who needs drama when you can have snakes (as long as you never actually see them, of course!)?

The Tin Man, watching over
Plas Glyn y Weddw

Pwllheli - Abersoch, July 21st 2023

Bus roulette: you never know where you'll end up! Mine dropped me off in a mystery spot, so I confidently marched "towards the sea"...straight into a dead end. Sheepishly returning to the bus stop (hoping nobody noticed!), I finally found the path and began my walk.

Promenade, golf course - pleasant but uneventful until Llanbedrog hit me with a rainbow explosion of beach huts. Leaving the beach, the path led past Plas Glyn y Weddw, a Gothic mansion-turned-art gallery. On the exposed headland, a lone tin man statue stood in silent vigil, gazing back at the beach.

The heather on this exposed mountain stole the show, bursting with vibrant colours. Descending the other side, the path dropped dramatically onto a beach. Soft sand beneath my feet, oystercatchers outcry, I trudged along, Abersoch my goal. But then, the path betrayed me, leading me to the bustling "Welsh Riviera." Tourists filled the streets and cafes, so I ducked into a quiet pub for a celebratory dinner. This marked the end of a long week, from Aberystwyth to Abersoch by foot. Awful weather, too many miles, I felt like a broken biscuit. I now had recovery time! August off, then back in September to chip away at more of this wild Wales Coast Path.

Porth Neigwl

Abersoch - Aberdaron, September 9th 2023

Back in Abersoch after the summer break, the lingering scent of the Eisteddfod festival in Pwllheli filled the air. Time to pick up where I left off! The path wasn't the clearest, and soon I found myself backtracking after mistakenly ending up on the beach. Admiring the (ridiculously expensive) houses perched along the cliffs as I walked up a lane, eventually passed the headland and headed straight for the beach – through a charming village of beach huts, of course.

Safe on the sand, my joy was short-lived as the path detoured through a golf course. Picturesque views of the lifeboat station at Penrhyn Du made up for it. As I walked, I remembered my farmer friend near Barmouth pointing out St Tudwal's Island, aka "Bear Gryls Island." Now, there it was, just off the coast! Lost in thought about what life might be like on that exposed rock, I completely missed Bear Gryls himself carrying bright blue tubs down to the beach. Kicking myself at another missed celebrity selfie, I moved on.

Reaching a trig point, I got my first impressive view of Porth Neigwl, also known as Hell's Mouth beach. Unlike the blue or green waters I'd seen so far, this beach had dramatic black water clashing with the white of the crashing waves. A surfer's paradise, no doubt. But my beach walk was brief, as the path whisked me away onto a lane lined with campervans.

Fields of cows followed, thankfully unbothered by my

135   *The Pig at Mynydd Penarfynydd*

presence. After navigating a maze of ruined barns and paths, I found myself back on the road, my boots thumping on the tarmac. Cars whizzed by, forcing me to jump into the hedges every so often. Finally, I reached a car park overlooking the same Porth Neigwl beach I'd been on two hours ago! Avoiding the steep track down to the beach, the coast path had taken me inland instead.

Through a pine woodland, I passed the grand Plas yn Rhiw house, though I couldn't even catch a glimpse of it, its huge rhododendrons with pink flowers in full bloom. The next part was a barren headland named Mynydd Penarfynydd. A quick stop at the trig point, then I reached the furthest point of the headland– and found a pig! More accurately, an art exhibit by a local artist. What a surprise!

Tired but determined, I continued, now walking on the road. A tiny valley full of big and bad cows loomed ahead – nope, not going there! Thankfully, I found a detour. With daylight fading fast (I'd been up since 3 am!), the path hugged the cliff edge, offering views of the two Ynys Gwylan islands – or maybe I was just too tired as they looked like the crocodile from Peter Pan, just its head showing out of the water!

Rounding the headland, the sight of Aberdaron brought relief. Reaching the lively village, I walked through in my boots, generously decorated with sheep droppings and emitting a fragrance that would make a

Ynys Gwylan.. or the crocodile from
Peter Pan?

skunk blush. I felt a bit out of place amidst the glammed up people enjoying their night out. Aberdaron marked the end of a long, tiring day, but a rewarding one.

139   *Bardsey Island floating off Mynydd Mawr*

Aberdaron - Porth Oer, September 10th 2023

Whole body aching from yesterday's monster hike, I limped back to Aberdaron for a gentler stroll. Five minutes in however, a mountain of steps smacked me in the face. Not ideal. Thankfully, a couple emerged ahead, like compass-carrying angels, leading the way along the meandering path. Not looking at my map every few minutes I get to relax, I just hope they know where I'm going. We reached a tiny cove called Porth Meudwy, a perfect spot for their rest break. Me? Seals! The joyful barks from Hen Borth beckoned, reminding me why I trudged through monster walks and steps-of-doom. These blubbery friends never fail to brighten my day. With plenty of time to spare, I soaked up the sunshine and seal show. Then onto Pen y Cil, the southernmost tip of the Llyn Peninsula. The wind huffed and puffed, but that panoramic view of Cardigan Bay and Bardsey Island took my breath away. The next two miles hugged the peninsula's edge, the wind created a whittling sound in my ears. Mynydd Mawr, the peninsula's southwest corner, appeared. A radar station platform offered a brief respite before the final climb to the lookout station. Wind-battered and burnt out, I trudged upwards. Suddenly, a man and his dog materialised from the car park at the top. "Is that it?" he asked with a disappointing tone, gesturing at the endless sea view. No fireworks, no carnival, just raw, beautiful nature. I smiled, taking it all in. It was enough for me.

Porth Oer

Rain sprinkled down, turning the path into a mini Pembrokeshire experience – down, then up, then down again. The coast path teased me with glimpses of Porth Oer, also known as Whistling Sands. Legend says the sand groans when you walk on it. With a childish grin plastered on my face, I stomped on the beach, and sure enough, the sand sang its strange, musical tune. As the sun dipped below the horizon, I knew this day, despite its ups and downs, was a perfect walk after all.

Porth Colmon

Porth Oer - Morfa Nefyn, September 11th 2023

Bidding farewell to Porth Oer's honeyed sands, a top 10 Welsh beach contender, my walk continued. Today fields were my home, each step unveiling another cove. Porth Lago, Porth Ferin, the list went on - seriously! I'm not making it up.

Reaching the longer Porth Colmon, a detour sign greeted me. Having missed the initial sign on the other side of the detour, I ended up facing a 5-foot drop instead of the expected steps. Pack flung down, a comical tumble later, and a dusty brush-off, I was back on track. Porth Colmon, a charming surprise with a hidden waterfall, offered a quick rest before I climbed out the far side of the beach, rain clouds looming.

More harbours followed, remnants of a busier past, now echoing with just my plodding footsteps. At Porth Towyn, yet another stunner, the rain held off, but Penrhyn Cwmistir stole the show. The biggest seal pod I'd ever seen - pure joy! As dusk approached, the heavens opened. My path meanders through a golf course, battling wind and rain until the lookout station at Porthdinllaen. A brief respite at the lifeboat station, then onto the fishermen's paths leading back to the beach and The Inn on the Beach. Leaving the beach, the golf course again became my final hurdle, wind and rain throwing one last tantrum.

145   *RNLI Porthdinllaen Lifeboat Station*

Streetlights flickered on as I reached Morfa Nefyn, daylight fading. Relief washed over me - the day was done. 26000 steps and countless coves crushed, soaked but happy. Another epic Welsh adventure in the bag.

Porth y Nant

Morfa Nefyn - Clynnog Fawr, September 12th 2023

I'm back at Morfa Nefyn, and the tide's in. The sky's a mix of blues and greys, kind of like the colour of a battleship. I hit the coastal trail at Porth Nefyn, which is basically a front-row seat to a beach that covers miles. The trail gets a bit more vertical after Nefyn, and it's a soggy mess thanks to yesterday's downpour. I'm talking about puddles so big you could swim in them. Nearing Yr Eifl, there's a quarry that looks like a scene from a post-apocalyptic movie—just rocks and rubble as far as the eye can see.

Then the path takes a nosedive, and after a bit of huffing and puffing, I'm in this snug and secluded village, the Welsh Language Centre. It's hiding between the mountains and the sea, like it's playing hide and seek with the rest of the world. The climb out is steep, and just my luck, the rain's back with a vengeance. There's some heather popping out in neon pink, but other than that it's just grey mist, mist, and more mist.

I hit the peak, the highest point of the whole Coast Path, supposedly the view's a knockout, but I wouldn't know—I'm basically inside a cloud. Heading down the other side, the fog starts to lift, and I get a glimpse of what's left of an old quarry. It's got the ruins of buildings that must've been busy back in the day.

Trefor Stacks

Back by the ocean, I swing by the Trefor Sea Stacks. I tried to snap some pictures, but the breeze was having none of it, so I gave up and stuck to the path. I make a pit stop at the pier, then it's onto the road. It's one of the longest sections of pavement on the path, people whine about it. Honestly, I'd take a smooth cycle track over trudging through cow dung if there's nothing to see any day. Eventually, I blindly blunder upon Ffynnon Beuno, an old well that's supposed to have some sort of magic mojo. Though, if you ask me, the only thing you'll get from it these days is a trip to the doctor. A hop, skip, and a jump later, I'm in Clynnog Fawr, where the village is tiny but the church is huge. Till tomorrow, toodle pip.

151   *Caernarfon Castle*

Clynnog Fawr - Caernarfon, September 13th 2023

Back on the trail, I returned to Clynnog Fawr the next day. The roar of traffic replaces the ocean breeze. Dodging cars on the main road, I long for a break. Then, a miracle! A friendly stranger offers a lift, but that would be cheating, wouldn't it?

Reaching Dinas Dinlle, The air is pulsing with excitement, likely due to the nearby airport. The seafront unfolds, revealing yesterday's friend, Yr Eifl standing proud, cloud free and Anglesey winks from the other side of the Menai Strait. Inland, a debate rages within me. Could that be the mighty Yr Wyddfa? Unlike the beachgoers gazing seaward, my eyes are fixed on the mountains. Leaving the beach, I pass the Caernarfon Airport, home to the Wales Air Ambulance and Coastguard helicopters. Eryri keeps them busy I imagine. Beyond the airport, peace descends as I walk the sea wall. Warm sun and a clear sky bathe the landscape in serenity. Hedges explode with butterflies, fluttering like a Mexican wave in the breeze.

The path dips inland to cross a bridge, then returns to the coast. A quiet road follows the Menai Strait, offering a peaceful stroll towards Caernarfon. The town's crowning jewel, the castle, dominates the skyline. It's a fitting end to this day, but the journey continues tomorrow.

153   *Mystery chimney in a housing estate*

Caernarfon - Llanfairpwllgwyngyllgogerychwyrndrobwlll antysiliogogogoch, September 14th 2023

Shhh! Caernarfon yawned awake, as did I. A noiseless walk around the town square and castle, still draped in sleep. It was bliss to have them to myself before the energy of the day kicked in. The Coast Path hugged the ancient castle walls, then pokes me through an archway into another world: Victoria Dock. A modern harbour that spoke of its timber-trading past.

Trading urban vibes for leafy tracks, I walked under a canopy of trees, sunlight dappling the path. My inner history buff told me this was once a railway line. Stomping through a housing estate with a random 50 foot chimney in someone's garden, I stole glimpses of Anglesey across the water, my next stop.

Under the mighty Britannia Bridge, the view wasn't grand, but the scale was undeniable. Emerging by the Menai Suspension Bridge, I found it bustling with repair work and traffic lights. Crossing it, the wind bounced me about, but the view was worth the wobble. Anglesey! A spring filled my step.

Losing the path in my excitement, I walked the road instead, missing the loop around Church Island. The water's edge beckoned, and this side of the Menai Strait was a beauty. Standing between the two bridges, I watched the swirling waters of the Swellies,

155   *Pont Britannia*

mesmerised.

Passing under the Britannia Bridge again, I was greeted by a quaint church and a Nelson statue. Further inland, another statue perched on a column piqued my curiosity. A little further, just outside Llanfairpwllgwyngyll, I called it a day. The unpronounceable town name might be a challenge, but the journey had been pure joy.

Rhuddgaer Stepping Stones

Llanfair Pg - Malltraeth, September 15th 2023

Anglesey greeted me with a noisy road, where the Wales Coast Path joined its island cousin for the island loop. I soon found myself on a farmer's driveway, questioning the path's logic. This wasn't the first time it led me past someone's front door or deep into a cow-filled field, miles from the coast.

This time, mud-caked cows and endless fences conspired to send me on a detour, costing me the burial chamber – the only complete one I'd ever seen. Time was tight, so I pressed on, enjoying the quiet country roads. The path split, high or low tide options. Unsure of the tides, I opted for high, hoping for speed and less sogginess.

At Llanidan, I crossed paths with some other walkers: a couple with their dog and two runners doing the path in the other direction. They took the low tide path along the shore. I've chatted with a few folks along the way, each with their own reasons and ideas for walking this path. It seems like this loop around Anglesey is more popular than other sections.

Fields gave way to the Sea Zoo, then a beach road before ending on the sand itself. Back into the fields, a mesmerising view across the Strait to Caernarfon. Then came the weirdness: a maze of paths culminating in the biggest stepping stones I'd ever seen, they must've been built for giants!

159 *As close to Llanddwyn Island as the path gets*

Newborough Warren unfolded, vast and pine-filled. But frustration gnawed at me. Why didn't the path take me to Ynys Llanddwyn, the iconic Welsh island lighthouse? Instead, it looped around the Malltraeth Estuary, hidden by trees. A shorter, direct route existed! Reaching the road, I recognized the woodland across the road, Llyn Parc Mawr – a red squirrel haven. A final stomp and I crossed the estuary, the sun setting on a long day, a long week. I had walked from Abersoch to Malltraeth. Soon, I'd return to continue the Anglesey loop.

Eglwys Cwyfan Chapel in the sea

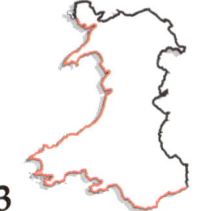

Malltraeth - Rhosneigr, September 23rd 2023

A week later, I was back at Malltraeth, the estuary shimmering and the new 20mph speed limit caused bus havoc. I started an hour behind schedule, already tired after the early drive.

Malltraeth's beauty calmed me down. Lush green and dotted with grand houses, the coastline expanded out like a welcoming arm. The first leg was mainly road walking, peaceful with minimal traffic. After Aberffraw, the path transformed into a coastal track, weaving through hidden bays.

A noise boomed through the air, like thunder rolling across the sky. An airport maybe? The iconic church in the sea, it had been a highlight on my mind since crossing onto Anglesey, and here it was. Luck was on my side – the tide was out, allowing me to explore the weathered marvel up close.

The noise continued, this time identified – motorbikes roaring around Anglesey Motor Circuit. The path skirted the fence, the rhythmic roar punctuated by the crashing waves against the cliffs. Porth Trecastell was surprisingly crowded, and soon I found the culprit – a burial chamber adorned with prehistoric art, shielded by a modern chamber. Unfortunately, the crowds wouldn't budge, so I pressed on.

Rhosneigr's south beach beckoned. A leisurely stroll to the north side? Not quite. A wide stream barred my way, leaving me stranded. Hope arrived in the form of a couple. If they lived locally, they'd know how to cross, but they too retreated. Undeterred, I scrambled through dunes, finally crossing a hidden footbridge. Rhosneigr swarmed with Saturday afternoon life – windsurfers danced on dark waves, a competition adding to the festive air. As the sun dipped low, casting long shadows, I knew it was time to call it a day. The island loop was taking shape, I'll be back tomorrow to tackle the next section.

Cymyran Bay

Rhosneigr - Trearddur Bay, September 28th 2023

Planning went kablooey. My meticulous order, shattered. Missing the bus, I found myself back in Rhosneigr five days later, facing the second storm of the week, Storm Agnes. Finishing the path this year felt like a distant dream.

Rhosneigr hummed with activity, even on this wet morning. A stark contrast to sleepy Caernarfon. The path led straight into a flooded sand dune area. Panic ate at my soul, tide times checked, hope dwindling. A kind dog walker pointed to an alternative bridge and drier path.

The other side offered no relief – a path disguised as a mud pond. Clumping through reeds, I finally reached the RAF Valley Airfield fence. Relief washed over me as dry ground rose, culminating in an incredible vista of the beach and airfield. The beach unfurled before me but the waves, monstrous and frothing, seemed intent on claiming it as their own. The sand, usually a welcoming expanse, was reduced to a mere sliver, barely a foothold against the churning sea.

My heart hammered in my chest. Should I risk it? High tide had passed, but the gusts grabbed the waves and lifted them higher. This wasn't the gentle lapping I'd encountered on other beaches. One misjudged step, one rogue wave and I could be swept away. The

167   *Scary waves*

thought of turning back, of admitting defeat was unbearable. Taking a deep breath, I plunged onto the sand, adrenaline coursing through me. The elements tore at my clothes like a kite, the roar of the waves a constant threat. Each footfall was a calculated risk, the sand treacherous and shifting beneath me. The narrowest part loomed, a gauntlet of crashing foam, the waves like mountains rising from the valley of the sea.

I ran, heart pounding, lungs burning. Would I make it? The ground sloped sharply towards the sea, the waves reaching out with grasping fingers. Just as the water nipped at my heels, I scrambled through the thin corridor of sand, collapsing in a heap of relief.

Reaching the other side, a fisherman greeted me, confirming escape was possible. The path then veered inland to Holy Island, where I met another walker, our maps and tans betraying our shared mission. An exchange of information, flooded paths blocked my way, forcing a detour onto waterlogged roads. Four Mile Bridge crossed, I followed the roads until they vanished, replaced by a farm track and a gate. More walkers materialised, sharing stories and camaraderie, a lifeline on days like this. Silver Bay offered a calmer atmosphere compared to the main island's beaches. Borthwen Beach roared with waves crashing against rocks as I continued, passing a National Sea Watch station. Catching up with a couple leaving the station, I learned the path ahead could be dangerous. At Saint

Treaddur Bay

Gwenfaens Well, indecision clouded my mind. Two more walkers appeared, their "not too bad" description raising scepticism (walkers tend to downplay challenges). Yet determined, I pressed on.

Slippery, green-slicked rocks greeted me, followed by the brawny breeze blowing in my favour. More crashing waves, more wading through flooded tracks – the path wasn't cooperating. Finally, tarmac arrived just as the heavens unleashed hail and sideways rain. Roads transformed into rivers, water cascading onto the beach.

Porth Castell, Porth Diana, and Trearddur Bay unfolded in quick succession, the yellow sand standing out against the dark sky. Exhausted, I called it a day. The path had thrown curveballs, but the storm hadn't broken my spirit.

Porth Dafarch

Trearddur Bay - Holyhead Mountain, September 24th 2023

Ugh. The bus wait gone wrong. I am waiting on the wrong side of the road! I waved to the driver as he zoomed past with my hopes of continuing my walk in order. No bus for hours. New plan: walk a loop up to South Stack and back via Holyhead, then continue from Rhosneigr tomorrow. Trearddur Bay is sensational, even through the grey storm clouds. Heavy wind and rain today, it doesn't seem like it's letting up.

Slogging up the road, hood flapping in the wind, I pass an ominous looking house straight out of a horror movie. Torrents of water stream down the road as I dodge pointless detours on the path that take me to the cliff edge just to bring me back onto the road a few metres later. Not today, safety first.

The wind and rain make walking brutal. It feels like forever before I reach the next bay. The waves are massive and furious, crashing against the cliffs. The path leaves the road here, heading along the edge. One look and I change my mind. Water washes over the path, and I'm not interested in getting swept away. Back to the road for me.

An hour later, I finally rejoin the path, soaked but safe. Reaching South Stack, I pass another walker, both of us exhausted and focused on getting through the day. A

South Stack Lighthouse

silent nod of acknowledgment is all we need.

Fog rolled in, swallowing Ellins Tower and the lighthouse as the wind howled to a new level of fury. A climb back to the road became a battle, each step a fight against the elements. A little further, Holyhead Mountain- the peak of Anglesey - the wind ripped at me, an unseen predator. My phone, my lifeline, went dark in my hand. No picture, no map, just the chilling realisation that I was lost, alone, on a storm-battered island.

A waterproof phone and a backup battery that normally lasts days, dead because of a wet charging port, no idea where the path leads from here.

No choice but to retrace my steps, losing another half day of walking. My self-imposed schedule is taking a hit, at least I'm alive to tell the tale.

Holyhead Breakwater

Holyhead Mountain - Valley, September 27th 2023

I never trust weather forecasts. Always wrong. But today, the uneasy feeling in my gut matches the dark clouds brewing on the horizon. I have to move before the storm hits full force.

A start before sunrise, Holyhead Mountain in a soft dream-like state. This was the squishy nice bit between the storms of hell that had been and were yet to come. Further West, South Stack lighthouse winks at distant ships. The sun's up, but hides behind grey streaks like a half-hearted tease.

North Stack – a surprise discovery. Its cave water glows an eerie, icy blue, and seals bobbing around make my day. Gotta keep moving, though.

Reaching Holyhead Breakwater Country Park, the view of its meandering harbour is majestic, a sharp reminder of the miles ahead. No time for a leisurely stroll; I'm driven, like a man fleeing a wildfire. This week's been a relentless wet slog, and I'm eager to avoid another drenching.

No scenic detours today. I bypass the loop out to the breakwater, heading straight down the road. Fortified house, closed hotel, the marina – all a blur as the rain starts, it's way too early! Luckily the wind holds off, a small mercy.

Celtic Gateway

Traffic rumbles by as I stick to the road. One turn and the tourist-trap seaside vibe melts into a teeming industrial port, so busy! The path zigs into town, crossing the Celtic Gateway bridge, then the chaotic train station. Noise, people, the rain's a constant waterfall now, and the wind plays catch-up.

Lost in the station's aftermath, the day disintegrates into a tumbling, miserable blur of rain and traffic. I end up on a housing estate, plotting my own escape. Soaked to the bone, every minute feels like the storm's punching harder.

Passing the hospital, I find a cycle track – a blessing, more direct, and tarmac under my feet. I'm not much of a runner, but today I dash, desperate to reach the finish line. Those last few miles through the Coastal Park, onto Stanley Embankment... they were a full-blown sprint. Holly Island done. Exhausted, battered and contemplating synchronised swimming if this weather keeps up.

179   *Porth Swtan or Church Bay*

Valley - Cemaes Bay, September 25th 2023

Bright and early, I started my day, back on the main island, leaving the houses behind. The ground was still soggy from yesterday's rain, making my boots squelch with every step. It felt like forever since I saw another soul, so when a walker came around a sharp corner, I nearly jumped out of my skin!

The path hugged the coast, taking me past a string of hidden beaches. Today was lawnmower day for some reason, the path maintenance crews with the loud buzz of strimmers echoing across the cliffs. This was a seriously remote area, with just a few scattered houses, no towns for miles.

After a few hours, I found a young seal basking on the beach at Llŷn y Fydlyn. The path then split - one way inland, the other looping around Carmel Head. As tempting as Carmel Head was, the threat of flooding and dwindling daylight made me stick to the safer route.

Sheep fields and quiet roads followed, with the path rejoining itself eventually. Then came another cow hurdle. Trying to avoid the main herd, I took a route that ended in a face-off with a bull. We were fifteen feet apart, me and this massive creature glaring at each other. Needless to say I backtracked in a hurry, like Scooby Doo backing away from a ghost.

Felin Gafnan

Safer pastures led me to Cemlyn Bay. The causeway creating a nature reserve was a torture chamber for my ankles - a never-ending sea of shifting pebbles crunching underfoot. Rounding the corner, I spotted the hulking Wylfa Power Station, a concrete eyesore in the beautiful landscape. To get closer, I had to wade through a shallow puddle, using clumps of grass as stepping stones.

The area around the plant was surprisingly lush, with thick lichen clinging to the trees and old stone walls. A few steps later, I reached Cemaes Bay, Wales' northernmost village. A geology trail explained the type of rocks found in the area, which I mostly ignored, heading straight for the harbour as the sun dipped below the horizon. The sky exploded in a fiery orange glow, casting long shadows on the charmingly crooked streets lined with old houses.

183   *Porth Llanlliana Porcelain Works*

Cemaes Bay - Moelfre, September 26th 2023

Dealing with public transport here is a bit of a challenge. They have a decent bus service that circles the island, but it doesn't always reach the coast. I always faced two choices: a ridiculously short walk that would've taken just a few hours, or a much longer chunk that would get me around the island in fewer days. Today was definitely a "long chunk" day. The bus driver almost choked on his Werther's when I asked for a single ticket, and seemed ready to turn away the couple who joined at the next stop! It turns out, we were all aiming for similar distances, nothing extraordinary, just a good day of walking.

We hopped off the bus in Cemaes Bay and I started my coastal trek. I passed by a church built by Saint Patrick – pretty cool right? Eventually, I reached Porth Llanlleiana beach with some fascinating ruins of a Victorian porcelain works. Up the hill on the other side, I found the remains of a lookout tower – the northernmost point of Wales. The Southernmost point seems such a long time ago, it was marked with a large imposing stone, but here nothing.

The hike continued with its ups and downs. I spotted the ruins of Porth Wen Brickworks on the next bay, but just as I got to a position for a picture, the heavens opened up. Thankfully, a rainbow appeared, painting the scene rather beautifully. I bumped into the couple from the bus again! We chatted about our plans,

Traeth Lligwy

swapped stories, and wondered why the bus driver doubted our walking prowess. It turns out, their app gave a much shorter distance for the same route than mine! Their company made the miles fly by, and even the rain in Bull Bay didn't seem so bad. They decided to stop for breakfast there, while I pressed on – a long day meant no food breaks for me.

Anglesey is sprinkled with windmills in various states of repair. I'd seen a few from afar, but the path took me right by a ruined one. Further down, I came to a flicker of the past: Porth Amlwch, the port that shipped copper ore from a nearby quarry. I wished I could stay longer, but the sunshine peeking through the clouds motivated me to keep moving.

More walking led me to Porth Eilian, a sheltered bay, and then Point Lynas with its imposing lighthouse. The scenery changed – rolling fields replaced cliffs, and sheep and cows became my new companions. I reached a quiet road with butterflies fluttering around like confetti and eventually emerged at Dulais Bay. Due to the open river mouth, I had to add a few extra miles to my journey, but it led me to two beautiful beaches: Traeth yr Ora and Traeth Lligwy. Daylight was fading fast, but I pushed on and reached Moelfre, passing the lifeboat station after the sun had dipped below the horizon. I tried to find the couple from the bus at Dulais Bay, but they were nowhere to be seen. Hopefully, they made it alright – some days, walks just take longer than you bargain for!

187   *When the path disappears and I consider a swim*

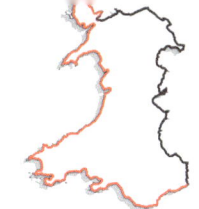

Moelfre - Beaumaris, September 29th 2023

Brutal last day on Anglesey! Moelfre might've been a good spot to relax, but nope, gotta push on. Through a caravan park and ended up on Traeth Bychan beach somehow (detour alert!). I lost the path, a dog walker became my hero, pointing me in the right direction. We chatted, and I could see the amusement in his eyes when I said I was walking to Beaumaris. 'Well done!' he chortled, a touch of disbelief in his voice.

Next stop, Benllech. Bunch of people milling about, so I shuffled through. Feeling good about myself, progress was smooth and Red Wharf Bay, a tourist haven, was soon behind me. Then disaster struck! The path just vanished – swallowed by the sea! Another walker joined me, we stood gaping at the path. Seeing the watery obstacle course, he decided on a shorter walk elsewhere. He did however suggest a detour that added a whopping 3 miles to my already overextended journey. There was no other option, so off I went on this sneaky extra route. Reaching the main path again, I couldn't help but glare back at the original spot. Low tide would've exposed a walkable path, lesson learned!

Another high tide route, follows a sea wall at Llanddona Beach. Road walking, a headland trek and then fields as far as the eye could see. Just mindless footwork – roads, fields, stiles, a manor house, a long field wall... Somehow I ended up at Penmon Point, the black and white lighthouse presiding over the sea.

189 *Penmon Point Lighthouse*

Quick photo op, then back on the road. Priory passed, Lleiniog Beach loomed. This is where things got ugly. The path directed me straight to the beach, a nightmare for tired legs. Rounded stones sinking under my boots, progress slowed to a crawl. Finally, the path rejoined the road – oh the sweet relief of tarmac feeling like a mattress! Limped into Beaumaris as the sun cast a warm glow upon the castle. Brutal week defeated. Now, excuse me while I collapse!

Beaumaris Pier

Beaumaris - Bangor, October 7th 2023

I'm on the final week of my journey and I couldn't have picked a better place to start than Beaumaris. The castle is a majestic sight, but the town has more to offer than that. It has a quaint pier, where I snap some pictures and notice the flood barriers. I hope they're just a precaution.

I leave the main road and follow a path that leads me uphill to a golf club. From there, I have a panoramic view of the sea and the piers of Beaumaris and Bangor. I feel like I'm on top of the world. I descend through some fields and a forest, and end up on the same road again. I walk along it until I reach Menai Bridge, where I meet an elderly couple. They ask me how far it is to Beaumaris. I tell them it's about an hour, but they look doubtful. Maybe I walked slower than I thought.

I soon find myself under the Menai Suspension Bridge, the same one I crossed to get onto the island. It seems like ages ago. I take some more photos, this side is a better angle. I also visit Church Island, a small islet with a chapel. I had missed it on the way onto the island, but now I can tick it off my list.

I cross the bridge again, this time on the opposite side. The wind is calmer and the roadworks are gone. I'm back on the mainland. After a brief walk on the pavement, I'm back to the wild coast. I follow the signs, but I miss one and end up under Bangor Pier. It's a dead end, but I see a squirrel. I get excited until I realise

Menai Bridge

it's a grey one. I'm not on Anglesey anymore!

I backtrack and get on the pier. It's a long one with a charm of its own, I can see why it won the pier of the year award in 2022. Just a short walk today as I'm trying to enjoy the last few days of this epic adventure.

Penrhyn Castle

Bangor - Penmaenmawr, October 8th 2023

Heading out from Bangor with the morning light, I felt pretty chilled about the road ahead. The only real hurdles were the twin Ormes, but I wasn't sweating it. Strolling past the quiet seafront, I bid farewell to Bangor without a backward glance. I skirted Penrhyn Castle, stealing peeks at its grandeur, then meandered through a nature reserve, taking a breather to spy on the birds. The coast was my companion, with the sea breeze for company and the waves providing the soundtrack. I made it to Llanfairfechan's swan filled boating pool and couldn't help but check if Penrhyn Castle still held its charm from afar, it does. The coast path soon joined forces with a cycle track, shadowing the A55. As the road burrowed through tunnels, I climbed for an elevated view of Colwyn Bay, while bikers whizzed by, probably puzzled by my pedestrian pace. After the tunnel, Penmaenmawr was my stop for the day. With the sun beaming and the sky a clear blue, it was one of those top-notch days made for walking. Just me and the path, no frills, no fuss—just the way I like it.

Conwy Castle

Penmaenmawr - Llandudno, October 9th 2023

The next day, I resume my journey from Penmaenmawr, following the cycle track that curves around the rocky coast. I hear the roar of cars disappearing into another tunnel, while I enjoy the quiet scenery. I see the traces of the old granite quarry, it used to employ many people in this area, along with it's sister Quarry, in Trefora. The mountains are still dotted with chunks of grey stone. My feet are sore, but I keep walking until I reach Conwy Marina. I look at the river that separates me from the town. It seems tempting to just swim across, but I know I would miss some interesting sights. Like Great Britain's smallest house, a tiny red building that once housed a fisherman. Or the majestic Colwyn castle, towering over three bridges: a suspension bridge built by Thomas Telford, a tubular bridge designed by Robert Stephenson and a road bridge. I cross the river on the road bridge, avoiding the traffic and away from the tourists.

I find myself in Llandudno Junction, where I follow the railway line. The path stays close to the shore, but I have to jump over some sand dunes by the golf course. I lose track of the path at some point, and end up lost on the streets of Llandudno. I wish I could see the sea, but I have to make do with the shops and the people. I leave the town behind and start climbing the Great Orme, a huge limestone headland that offers stunning

Llandudno Pier

views of the sea. I look back at the land I have covered, the island of Anglesey, the changing weather and the sun rays piercing through the clouds. I feel a sense of awe and accomplishment. I reach the lighthouse at the tip of the Orme, and turn back towards Llandudno. On this side, I can see a large offshore wind farm, and the faint outline of England on the horizon. I spot a group of people pointing at something in the water. I join them and see a few seals bobbing their heads. They look curious and playful.

I continue my walk and soon I see the impressive pier of Llandudno, the longest in Wales. I pass the toll gate and enter the town. The sky is darkening, but the lights on the big wheel are shining. I feel tired, but happy. What a great place to end the day.

The Great Orme with the Trig Point on Little Orme

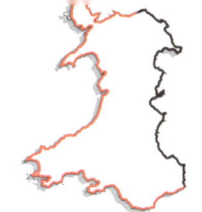

Llandudno - Prestatyn, October 10th 2023

I start my day in Llandudno, walking along the promenade with a few other early birds. The pier looks inviting but I have a long way to go. I follow the road up to the Little Orme, a smaller version of the big headland I walked around yesterday. I miss the turn at first, because a van blocks the sign. I backtrack and find the path, Two workers are busily engaged in repairing a gate. I greet them and climb to the top, where I see a breathtaking view of the Great Orme, the towns, and the bays. I take a moment to appreciate the beauty, then head down the other side.

I discover a place where magic lives: Porth Dyniewaid, a cove where dozens of seals are resting on the rocks. They look so peaceful and adorable, I wish I could stay and watch them. I have to keep moving, so I leave the cove and walk through a housing estate. I join the coast road again, which has a cycle track. I follow it all the way to Colwyn, where some construction work is going on. I have to dodge some barriers and detours. I pass the pier which is a shortened version of the great construction that once enhanced the foreshore.

I leave the busy area and walk along the coast, I can still hear the noise of the North Wales Expressway. It's a stark contrast to the quiet cove I saw earlier. The sound fades as I reach Abergele, where I spot Gwrych Castle on the hill. I remember that it was used for a reality TV show, where celebrities had to do all kinds of

Endless sands along the North Coast

challenges. I wonder if they enjoyed the view as much as I do? I walk by a series of caravan parks, which seem to extend for miles. This is a popular spot for weekenders from across the border, who come here to enjoy the flat beach and the sea breeze. I'm not sure where the boundaries are between the different places but I end up in Rhyl. There's more improvement work here and I have to follow some fences, signs and detours.

My coastal journey had already been a celebrity-spotting fiasco. Kicking myself over not recognising Gareth Thomas and Bear Grylls was nothing compared to this! Across the street I was sure I saw Ryan Reynolds. Barriers turned the promenade into a maze but I needed a selfie with Deadpool! By the time I navigated the chaos like a Tasmanian Devil, Ryan had vanished. A frantic search later, I spotted him at a seaside restaurant. Bursting through the door I declared, "Ryan! One quick selfie would be amazing!" The world froze and time stood still, a confused look came over the face of my hero and a quiet voice uttered, "Sorry butt, I'm Derek" My face matched the lobster on the menu as I slinked out, vowing to turn this into my new favourite embarrassing story. Rhyl blends into Prestatyn, where I reach my destination for the day: the Nova Center. This is where the Offa's Dyke Footpath starts or ends, depending on which way you go. It's a long trail that follows the border of Wales, but that's another adventure for another time. I stop here for the day, as the sun sets behind me.

Point of Ayr Lighthouse

Prestatyn - Shotton, October 11th 2023

The sun was already high when I started from the Nova Center in Prestatyn, the sky a canvas of unblemished blue. Today could be the day I complete the Wales Coast Path, with just 28 miles left to go. Despite the weariness in my bones from the past few days, the perfect weather bolstered my spirits.

The path led me to the beach, where the Point of Ayr Lighthouse stood askew, a painter dangling from it like a human pendulum. The River Dee was my companion for the rest of the day, its waters a silent witness to my journey. I passed a power plant, found myself on a road and then amidst fields. Nothing prepared me for the sight of the Duke of Lancaster, a beached steamship, this has been its home since 1979, its exterior weathered but its heart still strong.

Through fields known as The Marsh, which thankfully didn't live up to its name today, I walked. The Bagillt Beacon appeared soon, a testament to the community's pride in the Wales Coast Path. Next on the itinerary was Flint Castle, its yellow stones stood out from the other castles I had seen. I lost my way briefly after the castle but the coast path is forgiving and soon I was back on track. The Marsh returned, along with what seemed like the hundredth sewage works of the day. Then a busy road took me in its grasp for a few miles. The absence of signposts had me worried until I noticed the path's arrows and logo embedded in the

The Duke of Lancaster

pavement. Connah's Quay was a constant blur of traffic and students spilling out of the college at the end of the day.

I was grateful when the path led me away from the chaos and back to the tranquillity of the wharf. The coast path's logo was everywhere, on benches, gates, litter bins, even on a cage encircling a tree. It was comforting, a reminder that I was on the right path.

As I reached Shotton, the fading light made it clear I wouldn't finish today. Regretfully, I accepted that I'd have to return tomorrow. The forecast promised heavy rain but a brief respite in the late afternoon was all I needed. Tomorrow will be my last day, come rain or shine. The thought alone was enough to make me smile, despite the aching body. This was more than a walk; it was a testament to perseverance, a journey that mirrored life itself—unexpected detours, challenges, and the sweet promise of reaching a goal that once seemed so distant.

Jubilee Bridge spans the River Dee

Shotton - Chester, October 12th 2023

The final few miles of the Wales Coast Path awaited me as I returned to Shotton. The aftermath of the storm had left the River Dee a churning, murky torrent but it did little to quell my determination. With only five miles remaining, I felt an electric anticipation for the end.

Crossing the Jubilee Lift Bridge, a relic that hadn't lifted since the '60s, I stepped onto the tarmac path that would lead me to my destination. Puddles from the recent downpour dotted the way, but they seemed trivial compared to the journey behind me. The river now a straight channel, funnelled gusts of wind that cut through me, as if challenging my resolve.

At the Higher Ferry footbridge, I paused, drawn to the centre by an irresistible urge to gaze upstream. The wind was a force to reckon with, yet it felt exhilarating. Moving on, the river curved, and there it was—the finish line. My pace quickened, a mix of adrenaline and joy propelling me forward. I crossed the line, capturing the moment with selfies, the sense of accomplishment was overwhelming. As the initial euphoria faded, a reflective question surfaced: "What next?" Every finish line is also a starting line after all. As I stowed my camera, the piece of sea glass I'd found in Dale slipped from my grasp. Since then it has been my constant companion on this path, yet it doesn't belong here.

211 *The finish post*

A voice broke my reverie. "Have you come far?" I looked up to see a young couple, equipped for their own adventure. "Not today," I responded with a smile, "but it's been a long year." We exchanged stories, they were planning on completing the path in small random sections, I shared insights from my trek. Handing them the sea glass, I asked them to return it to where it belonged.

In that exchange, I realised the path had given me more than just memories; it had offered connections, a sense of continuity with fellow wanderers. As I left the path behind, I knew the journey was far from over. It was just another beginning, another path to explore, with new stories to unfold.

@JACK_WALKAHOLIC

Just one more thing.

870 miles – that's what we've been through. Thanks for joining me on this wild trek around the Wales Coast Path. It's been a journey and I've learned more about this beautiful country than I ever imagined. Picking a favourite stretch is tough but Tenby to The Green Bridge stole my heart. Anglesey's quiet north deserves a return visit too. As for beaches, Mwnt wins for me, thanks to those dolphins earning a bonus point but Whistling Sands and Trearddur Bay are absolutely jaw-dropping. Beauty is subjective, let's be honest most of us wouldn't travel hours just for a pretty beach, not when there's a diamond ten minutes down the road.

You don't need to be young or super fit to walk the entire coast path. What you really need is time, careful planning, and a lot of determination to keep going. Just don't let the path beat you! Let's not be sad because it's over, let's celebrate because we did it! This path isn't just about getting to the end, it's about the unexpected moments and the magic that happens when you put one foot in front of the other.

If you're hungry for more adventures, follow me on Instagram @jack_walkaholic. There's other paths out there waiting to be explored and I'm just about dull enough to give them a go. Thanks again for reading, Jack.

Milton Keynes UK
Ingram Content Group UK Ltd.
UKHW050043061024
449206UK00003B/9